A HANDBOOK OF
AMERICAN
CREWEL
EMBROIDERY

FRONTISPIECE. This set of bed furniture was the work of Mindwell Pease
of Suffield, Connecticut and is today in the Webb House at Wethersfield, Connecticut. They are entirely her work—she spun and wove the
background material and spun and dyed the crewels. Mindwell Pease
became the wife of Gideon Granger who was Postmaster General under
Thomas Jefferson.

A HANDBOOK OF
AMERICAN CREWEL EMBROIDERY

by MURIEL L. BAKER

CHARLES E. TUTTLE CO.: PUBLISHERS
Rutland, Vermont

Representatives
Continental Europe: BOXERBOOKS, INC., *Zurich*
British Isles: PRENTICE-HALL INTERNATIONAL, INC., *London*
Australasia: PAUL FLESCH & CO., PTY. LTD., *Melbourne*
Canada: M. G. HURTIG LTD., *Edmonton*

Published by the Charles E. Tuttle Company, Inc.
of Rutland, Vermont & Tokyo, Japan
with editorial offices at
Suido 1-chome, 2-6, Bunkyo-ku, Tokyo

Copyright in Japan, 1966
by Charles E. Tuttle Co., Inc.

Library of Congress Catalog Card No. 66–16722
International Standard Book No. 0–8048–0230–0

First edition, 1966
Fourth printing, 1970

Book design & typography by
Keiko Chiba
Printed in Japan

TABLE OF CONTENTS

LIST OF ILLUSTRATIONS

* All pieces in Plates 20–28 were worked by the author and are pictured in her home.

ACKNOWLEDGMENTS

MANY, MANY people have been of great help to me in the writing of this book. It would be impossible to name them all. Indeed, I do not even know some of their names, but their interest in American crewel embroidery and their hope that a reference book might be available to them has been an inspiration to me.

Very special thanks are due my late husband, Frederick E. Baker, whose patience, help, and enthusiasm was endless. Without his sure guidance, this book would never have been written.

My sister, Marion Lewis, and my friend, Ruth Latamore, have helped me in more ways than even they know.

Many thanks to Harold Pratt for the pictures taken in my home and my appreciation to Warren Blessing for his picture of the Tolman bed hangings and to Robert Blakeslee for the wing chair photographs.

To the Misses Louisa and Marion Billings, Mrs. Frank Cogan, Mrs. Reginald French, Mr. Elmer Keith, The Connecticut Historical Society, The Litchfield Historical Society, The Faith Trumbull Chapter, D.A.R. of Norwich, Connecticut, The Society of Colonial Dames at Webb House, Wethersfield, Connecticut, The New York Historical Society, and the Museum of Fine Arts, Boston, Mass., my deep appreciation for allowing me to share with others the beautiful crewel pieces in their possession.

And last, but surely not least, thanks to my publishers and especially to Mr. Charles V. S. Borst and Pamela Jackson Isayama for much understanding and kindness.

Muriel L. Baker

Farmington, Connecticut

A HANDBOOK OF
AMERICAN
CREWEL
EMBROIDERY

FREEDOM OF SPIRIT IN AMERICAN CREWELWORK

A GREAT deal has been written about English crewel embroideries, and there have been many fine illustrated texts on the stitches and techniques used in them. But relatively little has been written about American crewel pieces and their stitches and techniques. This seems a regrettable situation as there is a fine heritage of American design, and the stitches employed by our ancestors were well executed to give the desired effects.

Crewelwork is technically any embroidery done with crewel wools, which are slackly twisted two-ply worsted yarns. This embroidery is characterized by distinctive designs—some simple, some complex, some fanciful, some realistic—embroidered on a background fabric of twill, handwoven linen, fustian, or other material of similar texture. English crewel was usually worked on twilled linen, while American was usually done on plain handwoven linen.

The early settlers brought with them a knowledge of the arts seen about them in the Old World. They had in their minds pictures of how a few simple stitches and a few skeins of bright wool could change a plain piece of homespun into a gay chair seat, a bedspread glowing with color, or a set of bed hangings that would greatly enhance the plain interiors of their homes. They had in their minds a picture of the designs and motifs to which they were accustomed, but they were also aware of the great environmental differences, both in the countryside around them and in the interior of their homes. The embroidery they produced mirrored their awareness of this difference.

For example, American designs display a freedom of spirit that is lacking in the more schooled English designs. They are especially well suited to our modern homes as they are less heavy and cumbersome than most of the Old World pieces. Indeed, these American designs, developed from patterns and drawings sent or brought over not only from England but also from France, Holland, and other countries, were delineated to suit more nearly the way of life in this country. While there is no doubt that English embroideries had the greatest influence on American designs, we must not forget that the influence of many other countries was felt also.

Well-remembered curtains and bed hangings, heavy with great mounds, trees, exotic flowers, and fruits were made more simple, more open, more free, and more realistic. Whereas in England, for example, these splendid hangings were often the work of guild members who were so exacting about their work that if it were not properly executed it was cut up and burned, here most pieces were the work of a single individual or the female members of a single household.

If the embroideress lived near one of the metropolitan centers such as New York or Boston, she would have little or no difficulty in finding materials for her work. Early 18th-century advertisements mention such articles as "Curtains ready stamped for working" and "a good assortment of cruells well shaded." In 1743, a Mrs. Condy who lived near the Old North Meeting House advertised in the *Boston News Letter*, "All sorts of beautiful figures on canvas for tent stitch—the patterns from London, but drawn much cheaper than English drawings,—also Silk Shades, Slacks, Floss, Cruells, of all sorts, the best White Chapple Needles and everything for all sorts of Work." Another advertisement of 1747 mentioned proudly, "A Variety of very beautiful patterns to draw by."

It was, no doubt, to a shop such as these that Abigail Wadsworth went in search of patterns and materials with which to embroider. She made the long journey from Hartford, Connecticut to Boston on horseback. This turned out to be such a tiresome affair that when she worked her piece, she embroidered into it a small horse to remind her of her journey.

It would also appear that, in certain places, schools of needlework must have existed. There can be no other explanation for the great similarity of pieces known to have been made in nearby communities. Whether these were formal schools or just a gathering of interested folks about someone who was especially skilled at delineating designs and was willing to share her skills with others remains a question.

There is a much-repeated theory of how the early American woman, upon deciding to embroider, let us say, a chair seat, went out her back door, observed the flora and fauna with a practiced eye, and then returned to sketch them upon a piece of homespun, ready for her needle to bring alive. This was probably true in some cases, as the crudeness of the design and its concept can readily attest, but for the most part the designs were the work of a professional who had many design resources upon which to draw. There were prints, Herbals, Bestiaries, and design books such as Richard Shorleyker's *A Schole-House for the Needle* or *The Ladies Amusement* published by Robert Sayer. John Taylor, writing in England in the 1500's, tells us that designs for embroideries were:

> Collected with much praise and industrie,
> From scorching Spaine and freezing Muscovie,
> From fertile France and pleasant Italie,
> From Polande, Sweden, Denmarke, Germanie,
> And some of these rare patterns have been set
> Beyond the bounds of faithless Mahomet,
> From Spacious China and those Kingdoms East
> And from great Mexico, the Indies West.
> Thus are these workes farre fetch'd and dearly bought,
> And consequently good for ladies' thought.

Doubtless skilled amateurs were willing to share talents with others, especially in the country areas where access to shops was often difficult, and precious patterns were carefully hoarded to be passed around from one friend to another. But before the country worker could place a stitch on the material, there was for her, unlike her city counterpart, the task of preparing the background material itself—the spinning and perhaps the weaving. Almost every family grew some flax. In some of the colonies the growing of flax was ordered; in Connecticut as early as 1640 every family had to plant a small amount. So, the country woman probably prepared the flax for the weaving of her material, but quite possibly the actual weaving was done by a professional weaver, at least one of whom was in most communities. In one small New England town in 1704 there were four professional weavers who charged sixpence a yard for weaving. But even if the rural embroideress did not do the weaving of material herself, she most surely carded and spun the wools, as well as undertaking the exciting task of dyeing it into a pleasing palette of colors.

Many pieces from the hands of these country workers were done in shades of blue, possibly softened with either white or saffron. The reason for this is a simple one. Indigo was fairly easy to obtain, was relatively inexpensive, and from one dye color a whole range of shades from very light to very dark could be obtained. Even the white was swished briefly through the indigo pot to give it a pleasant mellowness! Thus, a piece aesthetically pleasing could be "wrought" rather simply and without using too many dye pots.

American embroideresses used fewer colors and fewer stitches than did the English. Their favorite stitch was a variation of the Roumanian Stitch, called New England Laid Stitch, New England Stitch, Economy Stitch, and a variety of other names. They also used the Outline, Herringbone, Satin, Flat, Feather, Buttonhole, and Running. These, along with the various knot stitches such as the French and Bullion, were all the stitches that she needed to give a pleasing variety to her work. When she wanted to fill in a large leaf or flower shape, she turned to these stitches in various combinations. It is unusual to find more than five or six different stitches used in any one piece of American crewelwork, and many times a whole bed hanging was worked in only two or three. Again, there was economy in stitching as well as in coloring.

The New England Laid Stitch was easily the most important of the stitches used in American crewel. It had two features that endeared it to the heart of the colonial worker: it was easily and quickly done, and it wasted not a bit of the precious wools. The picture (Plate 1) of a bed valance "wrought" by Eunice Brewster about 1765 shows clearly how little wool was left on the back. It also shows how cleverly she used this versatile stitch to fill every conceivable shape and form, achieving a pleasing variety in her work just by varying the direction of her stitches.

In this workbook are many representative units of designs. They show clearly the ability of the early American embroideress, her skill with design motifs, her way with stitches, and above all the charmingly naïve freedom of spirit with which she approached her task.

PLATE 1. Bed valance. *Courtesy, Faith Trumbull Chapter, D.A.R., Norwich, Conn.*

STITCHES USED
IN AMERICAN CREWEL

Back (Fig. 1)
Work from right to left. Bring the needle out a short distance to the left of the beginning of the line. Insert the needle at the beginning of the line. Bring out again at an equal distance beyond the point where it first started. Pull the yarn through. The needle is now ready for the next stitch.

Bullion Knot (Fig. 2)
Take a Back Stitch the size of the finished knot, but do not pull the needle through. Wind the yarn around the needle as many times as necessary to fill in the Back Stitch —four, five, or six times. Then, with your thumb holding the coils, carefully pull the needle through. Insert the needle again at the point marked X. Pull the yarn carefully until the stitch is even and flat.

French Knot (Fig. 3)
Bring the yarn out at the spot where the knot

21

is desired and hold the needle close to this spot. Hold the yarn down and wrap it *only once* around the needle. If a larger knot is required, use the yarn double. The next step is most important. Still holding the yarn, twist the needle in the direction of the arrow and insert it at X.

Coral Knot (Fig. 4)

Work from right to left. Bring the needle through at the right end of the line to be covered. Lay the yarn along the line and hold it down. Take a small stitch under the line and the yarn and pull the needle through over the working yarn. It is often helpful to pull the thread straight up, before moving on to the next knot.

Chain (Fig. 5)

Bring the yarn out at the top of the line to be worked and hold. Insert the needle at the same point. Keep the working yarn under the needle to form a loop and pull the needle and yarn through.

New England Laid (Fig. 6)

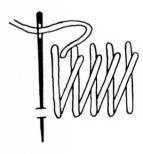

Always work from right to left. With the yarn to the left of the needle and the needle pointed toward you, take a small stitch at the upper edge of the shape to be filled. Keeping the yarn to the right, cross the needle to the left of the first stitch and, with the needle pointed toward you, take a small stitch at the lower edge of the shape. Repeat. The stitches should touch one another—they are spaced in the figure to show the technique more clearly.

Outline (Fig. 7)

Bring the needle out at the lower end of the line to be worked. Keeping the yarn to the left of the needle which is pointing toward you, take a small stitch along the line to be covered. This stitch is sometimes referred to as Crewel Stitch.

Stem (Fig. 8)

This stitch is just like the Outline, except that the working thread is kept to the right of the needle. The twisting line that results is in the reverse direction to the Outline Stitch.

Flat (Fig. 9)

Work from left to right. With the needle pointing away from you, take a small stitch at the top edge of the space to be filled. Then reverse the direction of the needle, so that it is pointing toward you, and take a small stitch at the bottom edge. The center ends of the stitches going in opposite directions should overlap, as shown in the figure.

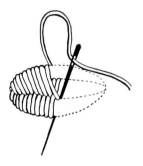

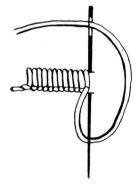

Buttonhole (Fig. 10)

Bring the yarn out on the edge that is to be raised. Insert the needle on the opposite edge. Take a straight downward stitch with the yarn under the needle. Place succeeding stitches as closely together as possible. This stitch may be worked closely, as described above, or spaced slightly apart. It is often worked in reverse to give a "spikey" effect to the edge of a flower or leaf.

Cross (Fig. 11)

This is an extremely simple stitch, but it must be worked evenly to be effective. First make a diagonal stitch and then cross it with another diagonal stitch.

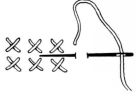

Herringbone (Fig. 12)

Bring the yarn out at A and down at B. Then bring the yarn up again at C and down at D. Move back a short distance and bring the yarn out at E.

Darning (Fig. 13)

Using the thread of the material as the base, weave the yarn over and under, exactly as in stocking darning. In early embroidery, the Darning Stitch was used in many different patterns—such as, over three threads of the material and under two. This is known as pattern darning.

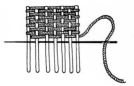

Feather (Fig. 14)

Bring the needle out at the top center. Hold the yarn down. Insert the needle to the right but a little below. Take a forward stitch on a diagonal to the center, keeping the yarn under the needle. Insert the needle to the left on the same level as the end of the last stitch and take a diagonal stitch to the center, remembering to keep the yarn under the needle.

Running (Fig. 15)

This is the simplest of all stitches. The needle goes over and under the material, as in basting, making the surface stitches of equal length.

Split (Fig. 16)

Make a small forward stitch along the line to be worked. When working the next stitch, bring the needle through the first stitch exactly in the middle, thus splitting the threads.

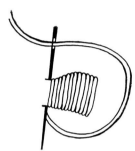

Satin (Fig. 17)

Work a row of Split Stitches around the edge of the shape to be covered. When Satin Stitch is worked over this row of Split Stitches, a smooth edge is insured. Carry the yarn across the shape to be filled and return underneath the fabric to the starting point. Be sure that the stitches maintain the original direction and are as close together as possible.

Star (Fig. 18)

This stitch must be worked evenly to be effective. Make a short vertical stitch. Then cross it at right angles with a horizontal stitch of equal length. Then cross diagonally in both directions.

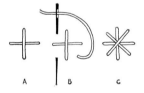

Squaring (Fig. 19)

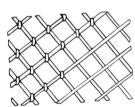

Take long straight stitches in parallel lines across the shape to be filled. Then take long straight stitches in the opposite direction, making perfect squares. Tie down these small squares with tiny diagonal stitches, making sure that they all slant in the same direction. The yarn may also be laid in a diagonal direction, as shown.

Tear (Fig. 20)
Work a single Chain Stitch. Fasten the loop
at the center with a small stitch.

DESIGN ELEMENTS

MOUNDS

THE DICTIONARY tells us that mounds are hillocks or knolls of an even or rounded outline. This is true in crewel embroidery. The mounds found in English embroidery are often heavy and piled one on the other, occupying much of the base of many designs. In American crewel, mounds are less heavy and are seldom piled so high. More often than not they show only one or two wavy lines, worked in the New England Laid Stitch. This was an excellent choice for working mounds as it is a surface stitch which leaves little wool on the reverse side. As the saving of wool was a necessity, this stitch was a favorite with thrifty housewives. In appearance it approximated the Long and Short Stitch, but it took much less time, a commodity also at a premium.

While mounds sometimes occupied only a small part of the whole design, just enough to support a tree trunk or a lovely flowing stem, they other times formed the whole base of the design. Very often the latter was the case with petticoat borders. These articles of apparel have some of the most interesting of all the early designs, often showing little scenes with houses, trees, deer, flowers, dogs, sheep, squirrels, and various other animals in and on the mounds. That petticoats were choice articles and highly thought of is revealed by this advertisement that appeared in a Boston newspaper in 1749: "On the 11th of November last was stolen out of the yard of Mr. Joseph Coit, Joiner in Boston, Living in Cross Street, A Woman's

PLATE 2. Bed hangings. *Courtesy, Misses Louisa and Marion Billings.*

Fustian Petticoat with a large work'd Embroidered Border, being Deer, Sheep, Houses, Forrest Etc. so work'd. Whoever has taken said petticoat and will return it to the owner thereof, or to Printer shall have 40 shillings Old Tenor Reward and no questions asked."

From an apron (Fig. 21)

STITCHES USED

    Outline: squarings
    French Knot: lower left unit; two upper
      units
    Cross: lower center unit
    New England Laid: lower right unit
    Chain: outline of each unit

COLORS USED

    Three shades of green: squarings; outline
      of each unit
    Three shades of blue: lower right unit,
      darkest at outer edge
    Gold: lower left unit; two upper units
    Rosy red: lower center unit

From a dress (Fig. 22)

STITCHES USED
Slanted Satin: entire mound

COLORS USED
Gold: lower row
Light green: two center rows
Dark green: two upper rows

From a bed hanging, 1745 (Fig. 23)

STITCHES USED
New England Laid: entire design
COLORS USED
Four shades of blue: lower unit,
darkest at lower edge
Saffron: small top unit

STEMS

PLATE 3. Bed hangings. *Courtesy, Connecticut Historical Society, Hartford, Conn.*

Of themselves, stems are not often the feature of a crewel design, but they are essential to a unified composition. Their stitchery, variety, and beauty are extremely important.

In American crewel, the treatment of stems shows great imagination on the part of the workers. Unlike English stems, which tend to the monotonous, the whole gamut of stitch combinations was used to make the stems effective and eye-appealing. Often in one piece there were many combinations of different stitches in a single stem. Here, indeed, was an opportunity to exercise one's ingenuity!

From a bed hanging, circa 1765 (Fig. 24)

STITCHES USED
Outline: center stem
Back: fronds
COLORS USED
Two shades of green: two longer stems
Light yellow: two shorter stems

From a bed hanging, circa 1765 (Fig. 25)

STITCHES USED
Outline: outline of stem
New England Laid: chevrons
Satin: alternate diamonds formed by diagonal squaring
Squaring: diagonal lines, laid in opposite directions
COLORS USED
Light green: diagonal squaring laid in one direction
Medium green: diagonal squaring laid in other direction
Dark green: alternate diamonds; outline of stem
Three shades of gold: chevrons, lightest at top

From a valance (Fig. 26)

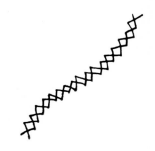

STITCHES USED
Herringbone: entire design
COLORS USED
Saffron

From a bed hanging (Fig. 27)

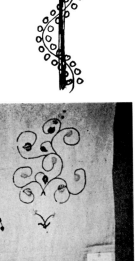

STITCHES USED

New England Laid: straight center stem
Outline: curving stem
Satin: dots

COLORS USED

Green: straight center stem
Light yellow: curving stem
Rosy red: dots

TENDRILS

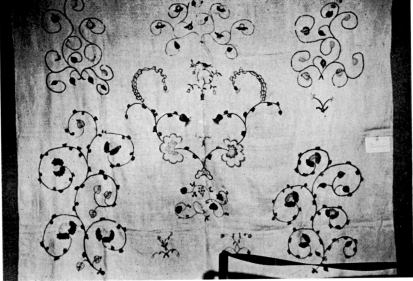

PLATE 4. Bed curtain (?). *Courtesy, Litchfield Historical Society, Litchfield, Conn.*

Strangely enough, these rather insignificant little lines form a very important part of the whole design. Often after an embroideress had finished a piece there would seem to be something lacking, some space that would look the better for a bit of ornamentation. And the curling grace of a tendril would just fill that need. The sweep of these curving lines would often contribute a softening effect to an otherwise rather severe motif and, in so doing, make it more pleasing to the eye.

From a bed hanging (Fig. 28)
STITCHES USED
    Reverse Buttonhole: tendril
    New England Laid: loops
COLORS USED
    Blue

From a bed valance (Fig. 29)
STITCHES USED
    Outline: entire design
COLORS USED
    Green

From a fragment of unknown use (Fig. 30)
STITCHES USED
    Running: entire design
COLORS USED
    Very dark blue

From a bedspread (Fig. 31)
STITCHES USED
    Coral Knot: entire design
COLORS USED
    Green

LEAVES

In crewelwork, leaves, both large and small, are as important as the flower shapes, and sometimes it is difficult to differentiate between the two! Here, the worker could display her whole repertoire of stitches and fillings. Here, she could experiment with the color scheme. Here, she could make certain that her design held together.

The various shapes of the leaves used are myriad. The so-called Queen Anne's leaf, a lovely curving design, was well thought of and embroidered in many different ways. The leaf of the carnation, which grew at every back door, was also a favorite. The oak leaf, grape

PLATE 5. Bedspread. *Courtesy, Mrs. Frank Cogan.*

leaf, maple leaf, as well as leaves whose shape never adorned a tree were all favorites.

Leaves were never detached from the stem or trunk which supported them but always fell from the main line in a graceful fashion. They were seldom angular but had sweeping curves that often bent the leaf to show the underside.

Small leaves were used much as tendrils were, to fill in any awkward or vacant spaces, and there was no end to the various shapes in which they were drawn. These small leaves were given the same careful treatment as were the larger ones, and because of this attention to detail, they contributed greatly to the success of the whole design.

LARGE LEAVES

From a fragment of unknown use (Fig. 32)

STITCHES USED
> Reverse Buttonhole: outline of leaf
> Star: design in leaf
> Outline: vein

COLORS USED
> Dark blue

From a bed valance, circa 1770 (Fig. 33)

STITCHES USED
Outline: vein; outline of leaf
Back: fronds
New England Laid: inside of edge of leaf
COLORS USED
Olive green: outline of leaf
Yellow gold: vein; fronds; inside of edge
of leaf

From a bed hanging, circa 1759 (Fig. 34)

STITCHES USED
Reverse Buttonhole: outline of leaf
Outline: vein
COLORS USED
Dark blue: outline of leaf
Green: vein

From a bed hanging (Fig. 35)

STITCHES USED
Buttonhole: outline of leaf
Outline: vein
New England Laid: lobes of leaf
COLORS USED
Two shades of green: left edge of leaf
Three shades of gold: right edge of leaf;
vein; lobes
Two shades of rosy pink: lobes

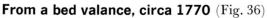

SMALL LEAVES

From a bed valance, circa 1770 (Fig. 36)

STITCHES USED
Outline: outline of leaves; veins
Back: Fronds
COLORS USED
Dark olive green: outline of leaves
Light olive green: veins; fronds

From a bedspread (Fig. 37)

STITCHES USED
 Outline: outline of leaf
 Weaving: leaf
COLORS USED
 Green: outline of leaf
 Gold: leaf

From a petticoat border (Fig. 38)

STITCHES USED
 Cross: outside of leaf
 Outline: outline of leaf
 New England Laid: leaf
COLORS USED
 Green: outside of leaf; outline of leaf
 Gold: leaf

From a bed hanging (Fig. 39)

STITCHES USED
 Reverse Buttonhole: outline of leaf
 Outline: vein
 French Knot: end of each vein
COLORS USED
 Very light green

FLOWERS

Flowers are the very heart of a good crewel design, and perhaps the most popular is the carnation. It was revered in England as the emblem of the Stuarts, and the spice pink was a welcome addition to many colonial gardens. The carnation lends itself to a great variety of stitching techniques, and it is interesting to note that it was not always done in shades of pink and rose. Carnations are large, and carnations are small. They are shown in both half flower and bud, realistic or fanciful—and they are completely charming!

The tulip, the potato flower, a passion flower of a provincial kind, the common daisy, the thistle, the bluebell, lilies of various

PLATE 6. Wedding dress. *Courtesy, Society of Colonial Dames, Webb House, Wethersfield, Conn.*

kinds, pansies, foxgloves, honeysuckle, clover, columbine, and of course the rose from its original Tudor form to a more realistic shape—all were popular favorites. The most often used of the smaller flowers were the anemone and the bluebell, and it was common practice to embroider a small duplicate of a larger flower wherever it seemed necessary.

And then, there is that large group of flowers whose origin is only in the mind of the designer. They bear no relation to any known botanical species, but they are rich indeed in pleasant curves and subtle nuances that tempt the embroideress. These unrealistic flowers were the backbone of English and Continental embroideries, and they never really disappeared from the colonial embroideries despite the trend to more realistic treatment.

PLATE 7. Pocket. One of the most interesting uses to which crewel was put was the decorating of pockets, which were worn beneath the skirts. *Courtesy, Mrs. Reginald French.*

PLATE 8. Petticoat. Another personal use was the adornment of elaborate petticoat borders, of which this is an unusually beautiful example. *Courtesy, Mrs. Reginald French.*

LARGE FLOWERS

From a dress, circa 1765 (Fig. 40)

STITCHES USED

New England Laid: edge of carnation; inner petals

Satin: dots on lacy edge; leaves at top center; calyx

Running: around inner petals

COLORS USED

Eight shades of rosy red: inner petals

Deepest rosy red: dots on lacy edge; around inner petals

Two shades of rosy red: edge of carnation

Two shades of light green: leaves at top center; calyx

From same dress as Fig. 40, probably a wedding gown (Fig. 41)

STITCHES USED

New England Laid: center petals

Outline: outline of lacy-edge petals; stamens

Weaving: lacy-edge petals

Satin: center of flower; ends of stamen

COLORS USED

Ten shades of blue: center petals

Medium shades of blue: lacy-edge petals; outline of lacy-edge petals

Two shades of green: center of flower; stamen

Three shades of rosy red: ends of stamen

From a bed valance (Fig. 42)

STITCHES USED

New England Laid: petals; calyx

Outline: separation between petals; tendrils

COLORS USED

Eight shades of rosy pink: petals

Six shades of tannish off-white: petals

Two shades of light green: calyx
Dark olive green: separation between pet-
    als; tendrils

From a bed hanging (Fig. 43)

New England Laid: all parts of flower
    not otherwise indicated
Herringbone: curving petals
Outline: outline of curving petals
Buttonhole: lacy petals at lower edge
COLORS USED
Four shades of rose: left side of flower
Four shades of yellow-gold: right side of
    flower below center curving petal
Two shades of green: lacy petals
Two shades of deep gold: lacy petals
Medium green: outline of curving petals
Medium gold: center curving petal
Two shades of blue: two outside curving
    petals

SMALL FLOWERS

From a bed hanging, 1765 (Fig. 44)

STITCHES USED
Herringbone: bottom leaves
Outline: outline of bottom leaves
New England Laid: flower
COLORS USED
Six shades of blue, darkest at bottom of
    flower

From a pocket (Fig. 45)

STITCHES USED
New England Laid: entire design
COLORS USED
Light gold: petals
Deep gold: center

DESIGN ELEMENTS **39**

From a wedding dress (Fig. 46)

STITCHES USED

Satin: dots at end of stamen; floweret
Outline: stamen
New England Laid: leaves at bottom

COLORS USED

Two shades of gold: leaves at bottom
Three shades of rosy red: floweret; dots
at end of stamen
Green: stamen

From a pocket (Fig. 47)

STITCHES USED

New England Laid: grapes; leaves
Outline: outline of grapes

COLORS USED

Purple: grapes; leaves
Blue: grapes
Off-white: grapes

FRUITS AND BERRIES

One motif that was dear to the heart of the early workers was the pineapple. It was the symbol of hospitality and was used either alone or as an accent with a grouping of flowers. Its colorings were apt to be rather startling in some cases, as realism was not considered essential. A blue pineapple can become quite a conversation piece!

Pears, apples, plums, peaches, grapes, and cherries were used in great profusion. These were all familiar fruits, and their natural coloration was pleasing. The grape with its vine was used over and over. Religion was a living concept, and the grape and its vine signified a laborer in the vineyard of the Lord. The exotic pomegranate, the symbol of immortality, found its way into many pieces. It has been suggested that fruit was often used to symbolize the twelve fruits of the spirit—love, joy, peace, long suffering, gentleness, goodness, faith, meekness, patience, modesty, temperance, and chastity. The strawberry was a new introduction on the market

PLATE 9. Bed valance. *Courtesy, Society of Colonial Dames, Webb House, Wethersfield, Conn.*

and as a rarity was thought worthy of being immortalized! Its cheery red would often add just the touch of color needed.

We can hardly pass by the acorn without a word, although it does not strictly fall in this category. Here was another motif used almost as much as the grape. It was easy to embroider and could always be depended upon to fill an empty space adequately.

Fruits as dominant motifs are more often found in American embroideries than in those of other countries.

From a petticoat border (Fig. 48)

STITCHES USED

New England Laid: entire design, with stitch direction different in each fruit

COLORS USED

Three shades of rosy red: each individual fruit

Three shades of saffron: each individual fruit

From a bed hanging (Fig. 49)

New England Laid: strawberries
French Knot: seeds in strawberries
Outline: stems
Reverse Buttonhole: outline of leaves
Satin: dots; small leaves at base of straw-
berries

COLORS USED

Two shades of rosy red: strawberries
Gold: large center leaf; seeds in strawberries; two upper leaves at base of
strawberries
Green: two large outer leaves; two lower
leaves at base of strawberries

From a bed valance, circa 1770 (Fig. 50)

STITCHES USED

Split: outline of each section of pineapple
New England Laid: inside of each section
Herringbone: leaves at base and at top of
fruit

COLORS USED

Three shades of yellow-gold: pineapple
Two shades of green: leaves

From a petticoat border (Fig. 51)

STITCHES USED

New England Laid: grapes
Outline: tendrils
Herringbone: single leaf

COLORS USED

Four shades of blue-purple: grapes
Off-white: stem end of each grape
Saffron: tendrils
Green: single leaf

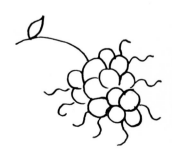

PEOPLE

PLATE 10. Petticoat border. *Courtesy, Connecticut Historical Society, Hartford, Conn.*

People were not often used as design motifs in American crewel. But when they do appear, they lend a certain dramatic touch— such as the man with his musket, proudly carrying home the wild turkey that he has bagged; or the prim little lady sitting under the arch of grapes, holding a little dog in her arms; or the startled shepherdess, looking for her vanished sheep; or Adam and Eve, often one on each side of an apple tree.

There is a certain liveliness that is introduced into the composition by the advent of a human figure, even though more often than not it was poorly drawn. An inspired worker in Montville, Connecticut placed a mermaid in one of the motifs of her bedspread. This saucy little figure added immeasurably to the charm of her embroidery. It has been said that the human figure was never placed on chair seats in the Old World because it was considered undignified to sit on a human being, but apparently no such feeling existed here. Two of the four chair seats, now in the Metropolitan Museum, worked in the 18th century by Mrs. Southmayd of Middletown, Connecticut, have human figures.

Figures are hard to delineate well. No doubt they looked very difficult to draw and too time-consuming to work, because time was as hard to come by then as it is today.

From a petticoat border (Fig. 52)

STITCHES USED

New England Laid: entire design

Darning: over New England Laid on bird

COLORS USED

Two shades of blue: top of hat; coat; stockings; New England Laid on bird

Pink: breeches

Red: front of coat

Black: gun

Off-white: face; hands; edge of cap; over-darning on bird

From a bed hanging (Fig. 53)

Courtesy, The New York Historical Soceity

STITCHES USED

Split: face; hands

Outline: hair; neck

New England Laid: all parts of design not otherwise indicated, with direction varied many times

COLORS USED

Gold: necklace; front of bodice

Red: lips

Three shades of blue: skirt; edging on skirt

Off-white: bodice

Green: edging on skirt

Two shades of brown: tail of mermaid; trident in hand

From a petticoat border (Fig. 54)

STITCHES USED

    Outline: face; hair; mouth; stems of
       berries; ribbon at neck
    New England Laid: dress; hands; mound
    Satin: nose; berries
    Reverse Buttonhole: cuffs
    French Knot: dog in lap; eyes

COLORS USED

    Yellow: curls; edge of skirt
    Rosy red: dress
    Off-white: face; neck; hands; dog
    Brown: eye of dog; mound
    Medium green: stems
    Blue: ornament on dress

*Courtesy, Museum of Fine
Arts, Boston, Mass.*

ANIMALS

PLATE 11. Petticoat border. *Courtesy, Mr. Elmer Keith.*

The study of American crewel is like a page of history; it is not a table of events or of dates, learned and soon forgotten, but a fascinating story of times past told in stitchery.

From earliest times, animals were used in crewel embroidery, and in the very early days of English needlework a great deal of symbolism was assigned to their use. The bestiaries were carefully studied, and often we find the human soul, depicted by the deer making its way through the hillocks, pursued by Evil, in the form of huntsmen who have with them all sorts of horrible beasts as well as the more usual hounds. The poor deer is beset with all sorts of obstacles, represented by snails, huge grubs, and perhaps even an innocent-appearing rabbit!

In colonial embroideries, there is less symbolism inherent and more realism. The animals tend to be deer shown in movement, dogs, little woolly lambs often worked completely in French Knots, squirrels perching precariously on a branch or twig, and rabbits hiding among the foliage.

From a petticoat border (Fig. 55)

STITCHES USED
    Flat: body
    Outline: outline of body; tongue
COLORS USED
    Off-white: body
    Black: outline of body
    Red: tongue

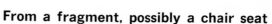

From a fragment, possibly a chair seat (Fig. 56)

STITCHES USED
    New England Laid: body
    Outline: outline and markings of tail
    Satin: berry
COLORS USED
    Three shades of saffron: body
    Brown: outline and markings of tail; eye
    Red: berry

From a dress (Fig. 57)

STITCHES USED

Split: body
Satin: hooves; ears
Outline: outline of body; tail
Reverse Buttonhole: mane

COLORS USED

Yellow: body
Very dark blue: eyes; hooves; mane; tail

From a petticoat border (Fig. 58)

STITCHES USED

Outline: outline and markings of body
Flat: body

COLORS USED

Brown: outline and markings of body
Tan: body; antlers
Red: tongue

BIRDS

PLATE 12. Bed hanging. *Courtesy, Connecticut Historical Society, Hartford, Conn.*

PLATE 13. Bed cover. *Courtesy, Faith Trumbull Chapter, D.A.R., Norwich, Conn.*

Perhaps there is no one motif used in the colonial embroideries that adds more charm to the entire design than birds. Here the embroideress was free to let her imagination run riot, both in drawing the birds themselves and in the colors with which she worked them.

Birds of all varieties, large and small, appear either as motifs in themselves or nestling in the branches of oak, apple, or pear trees. Turkeys, blue birds, peacocks, humming birds, and yellow warblers all appear in profusion, but seldom do we find an eagle. This would seem a strange omission at first, but this bird did not become our national emblem until late in the 18th century, and by the time its acceptance was widespread, the golden age of crewel was at an end.

The above pictures show an interesting feature often discovered in colonial crewel pieces. It is very apparent that the two birds in Plates 13 and 14 came from the same pattern source or were drawn by the same hand, even though different colors and different stitches were used in the working.

The bird in Plate 13 was worked by Mary Geer, and the one in Plate 14, by Prudence Punderson. Both lived in the Norwich, Connecticut area, where many beautiful crewelwork pieces have been found. All of the pieces from this area seem to have striking similarities,

PLATE 14. Bed valance. *Courtesy, Connecticut Historical Society, Hartford, Conn.*

as even the birds are alike, leading to the supposition that there could have been an active needlework school or group in the vicinity sometime between 1750 and 1790.

From a quilted bedspread, 1759 (Fig. 59)

STITCHES USED

New England Laid: body; comb; feet; neck

Weaving: head; second and fourth (from bottom) sections of wing; first and third (from right) sections of tail

Outline: outline of head; outline of eye

Satin: beak

French Knot: eye; parts of wing

COLORS USED

Four shades of rose: body; comb; tail

Four shades of blue: body; wing; tail

Four shades of yellow-gold: neck; head; beak; lowest section of wing

Very dark blue: feet; eye

Green: tail

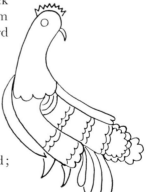

From a bedspread, circa 1760 (Fig. 60)

Reverse Buttonhole: outline of large
wings

Buttonhole: outline of tail; outline of inner wing

Darning: head

Outline: markings of large wings; markings of tail

New England Laid: top five sections of
body

Satin: bottom section of body; beak

French Knot: dots in tail; dots in inner
wing

Red: outline of large wings; markings of
large wings; beak; head; lower section
of body; dots in tail

Five shades of blue: body; outline of
inner wing; outline of tail

Off-white: body; inner wing

White: markings of tail

From a bed hanging, circa 1765 (Fig. 61)

New England Laid: body; parts of tail;
feet; legs

French Knot: dots in wings; eye

Outline: beak; outline and markings of
wings

Feather: tail

Three shades of blue: body; tail

Off-white: head; body; outline and
markings of wings

Red: eye; dots in wings

Brown: feet; legs

BUTTERFLIES and OTHER INSECTS

PLATE 15. Bed cover with quilted background. *Courtesy, Faith Trumbull Chapter, D.A.R., Norwich, Conn.*

These were used to fill empty spaces, and very useful they were too. While the colonial worker was not as afraid of open spaces as the English worker was, probably for having them all around her, she was wont to fill in the most glaring of them by the use of small leaves, small flowers, tendrils, or most happily of all, with butterflies or other insects. It is doubtful whether she attributed much symbolism to these—they were just pretty and useful designs which filled a need.

While the snake is not an insect, this motif, used so often in Old World designs, is not found in America, except as the serpent in the Garden of Eden. In its stead, there is often a trailing vine, sometimes with berries and sometimes without, that winds itself about the trunks of trees in a sinuous fashion. This device proved to be much more pleasant-looking than the snake.

From a bed hanging (Fig. 62)

STITCHES USED

    Satin: body

    Weaving: wings

    Outline: outline of wings; antennae

COLORS USED

    Dark blue: wings; top and bottom sections of body; antennae

    Red: center section of body

From a bedspread, circa 1765 (Fig. 63)

STITCHES USED

    New England Laid: wings

    French Knot: body; edges of wings

    Outline: outline of body; outline and markings of wings; antennae

COLORS USED

    Gold: wings

    Off-white: body

    Black: edges of wings; outline and markings of wings; antennae

From a bedspread (Fig. 64)

STITCHES USED

    New England Laid: body wings

    Outline: antennae

COLORS USED

    Dark blue: outer wings; antennae

    Red: inner wings

    Tan: body

FILLINGS

Fillings in colonial embroideries are much simpler and less fussy than those in their European counterparts. Fillings are such an integral part of English crewel embroideries that it would be hard to imagine a piece without a multitude of them. They were almost invariably used in leaves and other large areas. European fillings

PLATE 16. Bed valance. *Courtesy, Connecticut Historical Society, Hartford, Conn.*

were many and varied, some being very intricate in workmanship and others as simple as small Seeding Stitches. The other side of the coin is that their use in the great profusion that seemed to be the vogue sometimes tended to produce a very heavy and somewhat confused piece of work.

American fillings were simple: Darning, French Knots, Weaving using the threads of the background linen, small stars, and similar uncluttered units. This characteristic tends to give American crewel a pristine clarity that other work lacks. It is to the credit and taste of our early workers that they refrained from using too wide a variety of stitches and design motifs on the same piece of work. Thus they achieved that ultimate in good taste and design—simplicity.

From a bed hanging, circa 1759 (Fig. 65)

STITCHES USED

    Buttonhole: edging of four outer petals

    Weaving: second and fourth inner petals

    New England Laid: first, third, and fifth
       inner petals

    Squaring: circular center

Cross: circular center; filling of four outer
petals
COLORS USED
Five shades of rose: first, third, and fifth
inner petals; filling of four outer petals
Blue: second and fourth inner petals
Green: edging of four outer petals
Yellow: circular center

From a bed hanging, circa 1780 (Fig. 66)
STITCHES USED
Outline: outline of each section
New England Laid: all parts of design not
otherwise indicated
French Knot: center unit; dots in pine-
apple
COLORS USED
Two shades of rose: top part of pineapple
Two shades of green: lower part of pine-
apple
Medium green: all leaves; center unit

From a bed hanging (Fig. 67)
STITCHES USED
Outline: outline of each section
Bullion Knot: center
Weaving: outer petals
New England Laid: all parts not other-
wise indicated
COLORS USED
Gold: center
Three shades of light yellow: inner petals
Three shades of rosy red: middle petals
Medium blue: outer petals

MODERN CREWEL

MUCH OF the crewel being done to-day is, happily enough, being done in the traditional manner, but many of the lovely old designs need adapting to modern usage. Some simplification is perhaps desirable to fill the requirements of modern taste, and design units from several different sources can often be combined to make a pleasing new design.

The following pictures show crewel in use today. All the designs shown here were adapted from traditional 18th-century American pieces. These adaptations by modern needlewomen are effective and practical uses of crewel for today's living.

PLATE 17. Tolman bed hangings. From a design suggested by a petticoat border in the Museum of Fine Arts, Boston, Mass. These hangings were worked in New England Laid, Outline, Herringbone, and French Knots in shades of soft green and rose, to match an heirloom quilt. *Worked by Mrs. Frederick Tolman.*

PLATE 18. Wing chair, Queen Anne design. *Worked by Mrs. Robert Blakeslee.*

PLATE 19. This pair of wing chairs worked in a modern adaptation of an 18th-century design add a distinctive note to this gracious living room. *Worked by Mrs. Robert Blakeslee and shown in her home.*

PLATE 20. Box. Close-up of box in Plate 21.

PLATE 21. Covered box, shown on a Connecticut sunflower chest. Design of box adapted from a bed hanging!

PLATE 22. Bolster pillow. Design adapted from several petticoat borders.

PLATE 23. Crewel picture. Figures padded after the manner of 17th-century stumpwork.

PLATE 24. Chair pad, shown on an 18th-century bannister-back chair.

PLATE 25. Chair pad worked on handwoven linen. Design adapted from a chair seat in the Museum of Fine Arts, Boston.

PLATE 26. Pot holder. Crewelwork can be used for a modern utilitarian object.

PLATE 27. Curtains worked on 18th-century handwoven linen sheets, in shades of blue, rose, gold, and dull green.

PLATE 28. Valances, Queen Anne chair, and partially worked pillow in standing frame.

BIBLIOGRAPHY

Baker, Muriel L. "Notes at Webb House." Unpublished, Society of Colonial Dames, Wethersfield, Conn.

————. "Notes from Faith Trumbull Chapter." Unpublished, Daughters of the American Revolution, Norwich, Conn.

Cavallo, Adolph S. "New England Crewel Embroideries." *Connecticut Historical Society Bulletin*. Hartford, Conn. 1959.

Christie, Mrs. Archibald. *Samplers & Stitches*. Batsford, London, 1920.

Cummings, Abbott Lowell. *Bed Hangings*. Society for the Preservation of New England Antiques, Boston, 1961.

Harbeson, Georgiana Brown. *American Needlework*. Bonanza Books, New York, 1961.

Hughes, Therle. *England Domestic Needlework*. Macmillan, New York, 1961.

Little, Francis. *Early American Textiles*. Century Co., New York, 1931.

Nevison, John L. *Catalogue of English Domestic Embroidery*. Victoria & Albert Museum, London, 1938.

Wheeler, Candace. *The Development of Embroidery in America*. Harper Bros., New York, 1921.